This AMAZING book
belongs in the pocket of

Tyler Snyder

Written by Deborah Chancellor
Illustrated by Tim Sutcliffe

First published by Parragon in 2010

Parragon
Queen Street House
4 Queen Street
Bath BA1 1HE, UK

Copyright © Parragon Books Ltd 2010

ISBN 978-1-4075-8916-9

Printed in China

SURVIVAL

POCKET

GUIDE

PaRragon

CONTENTS

EXTREME EXPLORERS

So you want to be an explorer? Join a VERY cool club. Explorers are strong, brave... and a little bit crazy! They decide what they want to do and don't give up, no matter what happens.

Did you know?

Check it out

The Explorers' Hall of Fame:

- 1000s: Viking Leif Eriksson is the first European to land in North America
- 1200s: Marco Polo treks across Asia
- 1400s: Christopher Columbus "discovers" America
- 1500s: Francis Drake sails around the world
- 1700s: James Cook finds Australia and New Zealand
- 1800s: David Livingstone explores Africa
- 1900s: Roald Amundsen reaches the South Pole

Try this!

It wasn't easy for those explorers to hit the big time. Find out how they did it by reading a book about them, or looking them up on the Internet.

BE PREPARED!

Being a top explorer won't just happen by magic. You have to work at it, and that means planning everything down to the last detail.

Check it out

- Planning helps you think straight and focus on your trip.
- If you plan, you won't make too many mistakes or get lost.
- A good plan helps protect you from dangers and problems on the way.
- Planning saves you time when you're on the move.
- A plan tells people where you're going, and when you hope to get back.
- All top explorers plan their expeditions.

Top tips

- Check where you're going on a map.
- Figure out how long it will take to get there and back.
- Check the weather forecast to make sure you've got the right clothes.
- Find out whether you're likely to encounter any dangerous animals along the way!

Try this!

Feeling bored? Try planning an imaginary expedition to the North Pole. How would you get there, what would you take with you, and what scary dangers would you face?

SUPPLIES

So, you've decided where you want to go. What should you take with you? These supplies will help you survive for at least 24 hours:

Check it out

- Map
- Compass
- Water
- Food supplies
- Necessary clothing

Top tips

- Take layers of clothes, so you can add more layers to keep warm if it gets really cold.
- Water is heavy to carry, but absolutely essential—don't leave it out of your supply pack.
- Share the weight of your equipment with the rest of your team.
- Pick the right emergency supplies. They may save your life!

Listen up!

GRUB ON THE GO

Think about what food and drinks to pack for your expedition, and make sure you only take the best stuff with you. You won't regret it!

Check it out

- Bread fills you up and gives you energy.
- Sweet fillings in sandwiches, like honey or jam, keep you going.
- Cold meat, eggs, and nuts are full of protein to make you strong.
- Don't forget fruit—it's packed with vitamins.
- Fatty foods, like cheese or chocolate, give you an energy boost.
- Water is best for explorers—leave the soda at home!

Top tips

- ☠ Take packaging off your food—it will weigh you down.
- ☠ Avoid sugary snacks—they give you a burst of energy, but it won't last.
- ☠ Never forget water—you can't survive for long without it.
- ☠ Try not to take anything that will spoil quickly, or get squashed.

Listen up!

You may be a fast food fan at home, but this is no good on an expedition. Explorers need healthy food to keep them fit and give them energy to keep going.

WHERE IN THE WORLD?

To be an ace explorer you need to learn how to read a map. The good news is that once you get the hang of it, all maps are pretty much the same.

Key info

Familiarize yourself with the symbols for these things and you'll soon be a map-reading pro:

scale bar, hiking trail, road, highway, railroad, river, hospital, campground, forest, fields, mountain, ocean or lake.

Top tips

- Small-scale maps show huge areas of land and water. Large-scale maps show smaller areas in more detail.
- Remember, North is always at the top of your map.
- Groups of round lines that are close together show a very hilly place. These are called contour lines.
- Don't have a fight with your map— learn how to fold it away after you've used it!

Try this!

Start with what you know. You could look at a local map and plan a new route to a friend's house. How far is the journey? How much longer does it take you than usual?

AMAZING MAPS

Maps are great to look at, but it's more fun to make your own! Try to draw a map of a route you know well. Don't forget to add the stuff below.

Check it out

- Your home
- Local landmarks, like your school
- Roads
- Hiking trails
- Natural features such as a river, lake, ocean, forest, or mountain.
- A key to explain the colors and symbols on your map.
- A grid over the top (add numbers on the vertical lines and letters on the horizontal lines).
- A scale bar. For example: 1 inch on a map shows 1 mile on the ground.

Top tips

☠ Draw a rough sketch of your map first. It may help to look at an aerial photo of your area on the Internet.
☠ Remember how big the distances are, and try to get the scale right.
☠ Use pencils, so you can erase any mistakes.

Try this!

Make a treasure map. Hide some candy in a safe place, then write some clues, so your friends can follow your map to find the treasure!

"X" marks the spot!

ON YOUR WAY

If you get lost and can't follow the map, there are other ways of finding your way. Don't despair, just look around you!

Top tips

Try spotting a familiar landmark to help figure out where you are.

If you know which direction you need to take, use a compass to find North, then decide which way to go.

Look at the position of the sun in the sky. You know it rises in the east and sets in the west.

If it's dark, find the pole star in the sky. When you look at the pole star, you're facing north.

Did you know?

Animals, birds and insects travel huge distances, using their instincts to find the way. The amazing arctic tern flies _____ from the North to the _____ South Pole and back _____ again every year _____ 21,000 miles!

Listen up!

Always go exploring with a friend, never by yourself, and take a cell phone with you so you can call home if you get really lost.

LOST AND FOUND

Try not to panic if you do get lost—it happens to everyone! Many famous explorers have ended up somewhere different from where they meant to go.

Did you know?

David Livingstone was a famous Victorian explorer who was pretty good at getting lost. In 1871, he was found by his friend Henry Stanley, after he had been lost in Africa for six years!

Check it out

- In 1847, Sir John Franklin led an expedition to the Arctic and disappeared on the way along with two big ships and 128 crew members.
- In 1912, Captain Oates went for a walk in a blizzard, on a doomed expedition to the South Pole. He never returned.
- In 1928, Roald Amundsen set off to find a friend who was lost in the Arctic. Amundsen's plane crashed and he was never found (but his friend was...).

Listen up!

Give yourself enough time to reach your destination in daylight. It's much harder to find your way in the dark.

LOGS AND BLOGS

All explorers keep a diary of their expedition, called a log. You could write in a notebook, or type a blog on your computer.

Top tips

- ⊗ If writing's too much like hard work, try making a video diary.
- ⊗ Record the date and time of each entry.
- ⊗ Whatever you write, keep it short and snappy!
- ⊗ Be interesting. Say what you feel— be negative as well as positive.
- ⊗ Stick to the facts and don't exaggerate (too much).

My Log Keep out!

Did you know?

Christopher Columbus kept two logbooks; one was true and the other one was invented. He used the false one make his crew think his voyage to America was shorter than it actually was. This kept them from complaining!

Try this!

COOL CAMPING

You'll have to rough it as an explorer, so don't expect luxury! Get used to camping—most explorers sleep in some kind of tent or temporary shelter wherever they go.

Top tips

- Always check with an adult that it's OK for you to go camping.
- Never camp on your own—it's safer to share a tent with a friend.
- Use a campground, or get permission to put your tent up on someone's land.
- Choose a good spot for your tent—not on a hill or near a river.
- Take a good sleeping bag to keep you warm at night.

Supply list

You'll need to bring these things with you when you go camping:

- tent
- cup, plate, and flatware
- flashlight or headlamp
- sleeping bag
- cooking equipment
- food and drinks
- insect spray
- sleeping mat
- first-aid kit
- toilet paper

Try this!

Try camping in the backyard first, to see how you handle it. Do this during your summer vacation, so you can spend a few nights in your tent.

WACKY WEATHER

The weather can change suddenly, even in the summer, so you've got to be prepared for everything...

Rain gear

- ☠ Lightweight raincoat
- ☠ Waterproof hat and gloves
- ☠ Good walking shoes
- ☠ Set of spare, dry clothes in a plastic bag

Sun gear

- Sunhat
- Sun cream
- Sunglasses
- Plenty of water (Freeze some bottles before you go, so the water is ice cold.)

Did you know?

Scientists say that global warming is going to change the weather in the UK, making it more extreme. By the time you're a grandpa, it will be hotter and drier in the summer, and wetter in the winter. Snow will be a rare treat.

Listen up!

Always listen to the weather forecast before you start out. Don't forget that the experts sometimes get it wrong!

CRAZY CAMPS

Once you've gotten the hang of your tent, try something more adventurous! You could go to the woods and collect branches and other natural materials to make a shelter.

Top tips

- 🔥 Find a sheltered spot—it should be dry, flat, and away from a river or stream.
- 🔥 Get some strong, forked branches for the frame. Don't break them off trees, but find them lying around.
- 🔥 Ask an adult to help you build the frame, to make it secure.
- 🔥 Find lots of long, thin branches to cover the frame.
- 🔥 Grab a pile of leafy ferns to make the roof.

Ask yourself...

- ☠ Is it big enough?
- ☠ Is it dry? Cover the frame with ferns and leafy branches.
- ☠ Is it comfy? Put some leaves or moss on the floor, or bring a blanket to sit on.
- ☠ Is it safe? Check that your shelter is safe before you go inside.

Home, sweet home! →

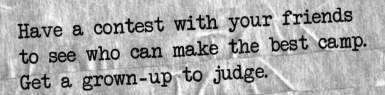

Try this!

Have a contest with your friends to see who can make the best camp. Get a grown-up to judge.

FOREST SURVIVAL

There are lots of things you can do to practice survival in the forest. You'll need to stay alert, and be up for a challenge!

Top tips

Laying and following a trail is a useful skill. Try putting down a trail in the woods for your friends to follow.

* Use brightly colored markers such as painted sticks.
* Take your markers with you—don't expect to find them in the woods.
* Put your markers far enough apart so you can see the next one in the trail.
* Don't spoil the environment—leave it just as you find it.

Did you know?

Wolves live in many forests around the world, and it's best to keep out of their way. They hunt together in vicious packs, and have a sense of smell one hundred times more powerful than yours... Yikes!

Try this!

You could build a small dam in a woodland stream, using rocks, stones and branches. Can you stop the flow of water?

THAT'S WILD!

You might want to go exploring to find a good wildlife-watching place. Remember to take a guidebook with you, so you can name the animals and birds you see.

Check it out

If you're lucky and wait in the right place at the right time, you may see the following:

- Deer
- Fox
- Coyote
- Rabbit
- Hare
- Squirrel
- Robin
- Bluejay
- Woodpecker
- Heron

Top tips

⚔ Before you start out, find out where the animal or bird you want to see is likely to be.

⚔ Wear dark colors so you blend into the background.

⚔ Take binoculars so you can see things from a distance.

⚔ Take a pencil and notepad, to jot down or draw what you see.

⚔ Be prepared to wait quietly for a long time!

Try this!

You could go to the same place at different times of day, at dawn and dusk if you can. You may see a different group of animals or birds each time.

CREATURE FEATURE

Some animals are more dangerous than others—they may be frighteningly fierce, or deadly poisonous. Even the boldest explorer should leave them alone...

Did you know?

The golden poison frog is the most poisonous land animal in the world. Just one gram of pure poison from its skin is enough to kill two million people.

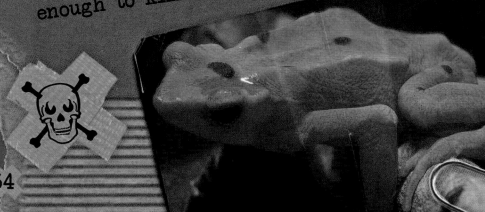

Top ten

Animal:	Number of people killed every year (roughly):
1. Mosquito	→ 1 million people
2. Snake	→ 125,000 people
3. Scorpion	→ 2,000 people
4. Big cat	→ 800 people
5. Crocodile	→ 800 people
6. Elephant	→ 500 people
7. Hippo	→ 150 people
8. Jellyfish	→ 100 people
9. Shark	→ 100 people
10. Bear	→ 10 people

Listen up

If you know that an animal is dangerous, don't go near it. If you're bitten by something poisonous, get help as soon as you can.

BELIEVE IT OR NOT

From time to time, explorers go in search of weird and wonderful creatures, hoping to catch a glimpse of them.

Did you know?

Some people believe that that a mysterious monster lives in Loch Ness, a Scottish lake. They say that "Nessie" is a kind of giant, swimming reptile and descended from dinos. Cool!

Top ten

Wanna go searching for the world's top ten crazy creatures? Here's where you might find them...

1. Loch Ness Monster, Scotland

2. Bigfoot, United States

3. Yeti, a.k.a. "The Abominable Snowman," Himalayas

4. Chupacabra, North and South America

5. Ogopogo, Canada

6. Lake Champlain monster, a.k.a. "Champ," United States

7. Beast of Bodmin, England

8. Dragon, China

9. Sea monster, deep oceans

10. Mermaids, rocky seas

GO GREEN

When you're out exploring, make sure you respect the environment. Don't drop a trail of litter and always leave the countryside as you find it.

Top tip

Take an empty plastic bag with you, to carry all your litter home. Remember, the countryside's not just for you, it's for everyone.

Outdoor code

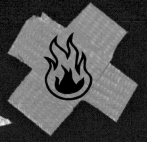

Here are some rules to remember when you're outdoors. They'll help you be a better, and more considerate, explorer.

1. Be safe.
2. Plan ahead.
3. Follow signs—don't ignore them.
4. Leave gates as you find them—either open or shut.
5. Leave land and buildings as you find them—don't damage property.
6. Protect plants—don't pick them.
7. Protect animals—don't frighten them or put them in danger.
8. Keep dogs under control.
9. Don't drop litter.
10. Be aware of other people.

PLAY SAFE

Being brave doesn't mean being stupid. There are ways of staying safe when you go exploring. Think carefully before you do anything that might be dangerous.

Keep out!

Stay away from: busy roads, railroad tracks, bridges, abandoned buildings, construction sites, electricity cables, gas pipes, private land, barbed-wire fences, fast-flowing rivers, deep lakes or reservoirs, deep caves.

Top tips

- Always take a friend with you.
- Tell someone where you're going and when you expect to get back.
- Take a cell phone.
- Don't talk to or accept a ride from a stranger.
- Don't go near deep water.
- Stay on marked trails.
- Use your common sense: if something looks unsafe, it probably is.

Listen up

Never go along with friends who are doing something dangerous, even if they laugh at you or call you names. They're not good friends if they do that.

DISASTER ZONE

Listen up

If an earthquake
happens, try to get
outside. If you're
stuck in a building,
go upstairs. It will
be easier for rescuers
to get you out if the
building collapses.

Top ten

Where are the world's most dangerous
natural disaster zones? Here...

Where?		Why?
1. Pacific Ocean	⟶	"Ring of Fire"
2. Central Asia	⟶	earthquakes
3. Bangladesh	⟶	cyclones, earthquakes, and volcanoes
4. South Asia	⟶	floods
5. Southeast Asia	⟶	tsunamis
6. Indonesia	⟶	volcanoes
7. Australia	⟶	wildfires
8. Southwest America	⟶	earthquakes
9. Central America and Caribbean	⟶	hurricanes
10. American Midwest	⟶	tornadoes

COPYCAT DANGER

Don't copy your ultimate explorer hero without proper training. Never attempt something you're not sure about—you need to learn the skills first.

Ask the expert

Ask an expert to show you how to...

- ☠ Use a sharp tool
- ☠ Make a campfire
- ☠ Cook a basic meal
- ☠ Practice self-defense
- ☠ Swim in rough water
- ☠ Paddle a kayak
- ☠ Go caving
- ☠ Climb a rocky cliff
- ☠ Rappel down a sheer drop

Top tips

- Never try to build or light a fire without asking a grown-up to help.
- "Wild camping" means camping in the open country, not on a campsite. Don't do this without an adult.
- If you're trying something ambitious, make sure you've got expert backup.

Listen up

Join an organization like the Scouts, where you can learn some basic skills, and have fun being outdoors with friends.

SUPER SKILLS

Don't worry about what you can't do—start learning something new today! Talk your friends into doing it with you if you want company.

Check it out

How many of these super skills can you master, to become a top explorer?

☠ Map reading
☠ Reading a compass
☠ Putting up a tent
☠ First aid
☠ Fitness training
☠ Swimming
☠ Orienteering
☠ Mountain biking

Top tips

- 🔥 You can't learn a new skill quickly! Be patient.
- 🔥 Don't give up if you find that learning something new is hard. Keep trying.
- 🔥 Take a friend with you to your new class or club, so you can encourage each other.
- 🔥 Make a video diary of your progress, so you can see how much you've learned.

Listen up

Even famous explorers have to pick up new skills. Don't be embarrassed about doing something new. Have fun and enjoy yourself.

ARCTIC ADVENTURES

In Antarctica, winds howl at up to 200 mph and temperatures plunge to -129°F. It's the windiest, coldest place on the planet. Feel like visiting?

Did you know?

In 1911, two teams of explorers raced to be the first to reach the South Pole. Robert Peary's team was better prepared, and got there first. Robert Scott's team used sleds that got bogged down in the snow, so they lost. Everyone in the losing team died on the way back.

Top tips

- 🔥 Always take the right gear on a polar expedition.
- 🔥 Wear layers of protective clothing and strong snow boots.
- 🔥 Eat foods that will boost your energy levels.
- 🔥 If things go wrong, huddle together to keep warm.

Listen up

If you meet a polar bear in the Arctic, run for your life! Polar bears can run up to 25 mph. And they have VERY long, sharp claws...

DESERT DRAMAS

If you decide to go trekking through a desert, don't forget to take enough water with you, or you won't survive for long...

Did you know?

Camels are used by travelers in the desert, because they are good at carrying heavy loads, and they can live for about two weeks without water.

Top tips

If you're unlucky enough to get lost in a desert, remember these tips:

✖ Ration your water supplies immediately.

✖ Shelter from the sun during the day in the shade of a rock or cactus.

✖ Walk at night, when it's cooler—this uses less energy.

✖ Beware of mirages—tricks of the light that make you think there's water in the distance.

Listen up

In a sandstorm, it's vital to cover yourself from head to toe, to stop sand from getting into your eyes, ears, and mouth. Yuck!

JUNGLE TROUBLE

The jungle sounds like fun to explore, full of amazing wildlife and hidden treasures. But watch out—it's easy to get lost! Everything looks the same, and the leafy plants make it impossible to see far ahead.

Did you know?

In 1925, an eccentric British explorer called Percy Fawcett went in search of an ancient city in the Amazon jungle, which he called "City of X." He was never seen again.

Top tips

Many dangerous animals lurk in the jungle. Follow our advice to protect yourself...

- At night, cover your whole body to protect it from mosquito bites. Don't forget your hands.
- Keep your shoes and clothes off the ground, so nasty insects, scorpions, and snakes can't creep into them.
- If you find a poisonous snake, don't attack it, but let it escape.
- Never swim in shark-infested waters, no matter how hot you are!

MOUNTAIN MISSION

Some explorers are addicted to climbing mountains. It can be very dangerous and extremely exhausting, but there is one big payoff—you get a great view at the top!

Top tips

Check it out

Listen up

If you can, stick to shady areas when you are climbing a mountain. An avalanche can start when the sun melts snow on a mountain slope.

STORMY SEAS

In the past, many explorers died at sea, on their way to discovering new lands. The open ocean can still be a dangerous place, especially during a big storm.

Top tips

If your ship sinks and there are no lifeboats, stay calm and do the following:

- ☠ Climb out of the water onto a floating bit of wreckage.
- ☠ Cover your body to protect yourself from the sun or cold.
- ☠ Figure out the best way to attract rescuers, and don't waste energy shouting (unless you can actually see someone to shout at!).
- ☠ Ration all your food and water.
- ☠ If you spot land, paddle in that direction.

Did you know?

The best way to survive a shark attack is to hit the shark very hard, aiming for its eyes or gills. Hopefully, this will make the shark back off. Unfortunately, playing dead won't do the trick!

Listen up

It is very important to learn to swim, even if you are not planning to explore the high seas. If you can already swim, take lessons in lifesaving. You never know when it might come in handy...

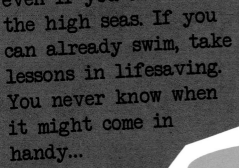

FLASH FLOODS

Sometimes, floods happen quickly and without much warning. They can catch anyone off guard—even the most intrepid explorer. As always, the answer is to be prepared, and know what to do if disaster strikes.

Check it out

How to avoid getting stuck in a flood:

- Head for high ground and keep away from low valleys.
- Rivers and streams can burst their banks, so don't go too near them in heavy rain.
- If your car breaks down in a flood, get out quickly, or you may be swept away.
- Climb a tree if you have to, and wait to be rescued!

Top tips

If you're trapped indoors in a flood, get help to do these things:

- ☠ Turn off the gas and electricity.
- ☠ Take everything you really need upstairs, e.g. food, drink, and clothes.
- ☠ Climb up onto the roof if you have to (but don't take any silly risks).
- ☠ Stay where you are until you're rescued, or until the flood waters go down.

Try this!

You could practise getting what you need upstairs.

REAL-LIFE HEROES

Many expeditions end in a flash of glory, with the hero's name in the record books. But when things go pear-shaped, people show how brave they are by finding a way to survive—often against the odds.

Check it out

- In 1914, Ernest Shackleton led his men to safety when their ship got stuck in ice in the Antarctic.
- In 1970, the crew of Apollo 13 escaped disaster by steering their damaged spacecraft back to Earth.
- In 1972, the Uruguay rugby team was flying to a game when their plane crashed in the Andes mountains. The survivors were rescued ten weeks later.

Did you know?

You don't have to be a grown-up to be a hero—all it takes is guts and determination. In 2006, 15-year-old Jordan Maguire from Scotland became the youngest person to walk to the North Pole. Beat that!

Listen up

Remember—if you don't reach your goal, it's not a disaster. The important thing is to stay calm and keep going!

SURVIVAL STORIES

Explorers who survive when things go wrong often have incredible tales to tell. Often, they were very lucky, as well as quick-thinking and resourceful.

Did you know?

In 1815, a boat was damaged in a storm near Japan. Two Japanese sailors drifted all the way across the Pacific Ocean before they were rescued off the coast of California, 484 days later.

Check it out

- In 1971, Juliane Koepcke was the only survivor of a plane crash in a rainforest in Peru. She trekked through the jungle for nine days to find help.
- Mark Inglis and Phil Doole were climbing in New Zealand in 1982, when they got caught in a blizzard. They dug an ice cave and waited for two weeks, until they were rescued.
- In 2006, Ricky Megee was lost in the Australian outback for ten weeks, and survived on a diet of leeches, grasshoppers, and frogs.

Listen up

Don't let these survival stories discourage you from exploring... Be inspired by them, and remember that no matter what happens, the best explorers never give up!

When I'm a famous explorer, I'm going to...